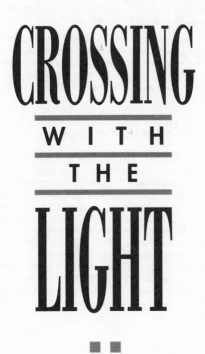

CROSSING
WITH
THE
LIGHT

*Dwight
Okita*

TIA CHUCHA PRESS
Chicago

ACKNOWLEDGMENTS

Poems in this book have appeared in the following magazines, periodicals, and anthologies: *Another Chicago Magazine, Banyan Anthology 2, Chicago Tribune, Nit & Wit, Off The Rocks* and *Pegasus.*

"In Response to Executive Order 9066" has been anthologized in: *Braided Lives* (Minnesota Humanities Commission), *Breaking Silence: An Anthology of Contemporary Asian American Poets* (Greenfield Review Press), *Crossing Cultures* (MacMillan), *Elements of Literature* (Holt, Rinehart and Winston), *Literature & Language* (McDougal-Littell), and *New Worlds of Literature* (WW Norton).

"Smuggling Poetry into the Theater" contains monologs from my stage plays: DREAM/FAST, THE RAINY SEASON, and LETTERS I NEVER WROTE.

Thanks to Luis Rodriguez for believing in this book, to Joseph Bruchac of Greenfield Review Press for acting as my unofficial agent for the past decade and forwarding requests to reprint "In Response to Executive Order 9066" to me, to Mary Shen Barnidge who was the first editor to publish my work, to Frank Schulz and Charlene Sens Gorius for inspiring me with their unforgettable friendship, to the Illinois Arts Council for the fellowship in poetry in 1988, to Marlene Zuccaro of Zebra Crossing Theater for finding a place on stage for my poems, to Curt Columbus of Victory Gardens Theater for believing in the poetic language of my plays, to John Frederick Nims for teaching me to shake the loose words from the page, to Diane Korhonen for teaching me to keep a journal in high school, to all my friends who chant Nam Myoho Renge Kyo toward world peace, to my mother for her unconditional love and support, and most of all to the audiences who've come to see my poetry performances and theater work through the years.

Design: Jane Kremsreiter
Typesetting: Susan Dühl
Front Cover Photo: Jennifer Girard (from the poetry video "Crossing with the Light")

Printed in the United States

ISBN 0-9624287-9-5
Library of Congress Catalog Card Number: 92-64247

Published by:

Tia Chucha Press
A Project of the Guild Complex
PO Box 476969
Chicago IL 60647
312-252-5321

This project is partially supported by a grant from the City of Chicago Department of Cultural Affairs and the Illinois Arts Council Access Program.

CONTENTS

What I wanted was so small:
to be able to enter any room
with a story to tell.

TO
WALK
ACROSS
A
ROOM

My Next Life

In my next life
I want to be Puerto Rican.
Like the woman at the New Year's Eve Party
in black mesh stockings pointing
at her heart saying, I dance from here.
I want to dance from there, too.
To talk with my hands and throw
large parties, to do even the smallest things
passionately.

A young man coming into his own, you said of me
and in my head I saw seedless green grapes
drifting in a glass of icewater on a terrace,
a grand piano I could press my fingers against
when I am lonely. And big parties:
celery stalks swirling on glass platters,
staircases to descend from—everyone
I have ever loved climbing down them:
forgiven, delivered.

Why put off until the next life
what you can do in this one? I gather
my friends in groups of six at our
regular restaurant—the one
with spoons scattered beneath the table.
Our cups lie face down on their saucers
as if they don't hear a word
we are saying, and the waitress watches us
from the kitchen through the window
of the swinging door. We will give her
something to watch.

1 ::

At night, the coffeepot stands upended in the rack.
A nightlight turns its seashell back to the room
and spreads its light on a wall.
Rubberbands hang around a doorknob.
These are the Certain Hours and for a while I know
where I stand in a house, I'm sure of it.
But then the coffeepot rights itself
and begins singing the old song. My feet lower
to the inevitable wood floor, to the new day.
All year, I have practiced this jump.

Parachute

2 ::

Frank and I sit on the swings in an empty schoolyard
tonight. We face opposite ways and he watches me
as we meet at the bottom of our arcs, watches me
get smaller and farther away. I slow, let the rubber seat
slide up under the back of my knees, hang there
looking at my shoes, stars. So what's your story? he says
hanging low in his seat like me.
I have no story, I say and look at the blacktop moving
beneath me, watch Frank getting smaller
and farther away.
I have no story. I have these chains and I hold them.

3 ::

They say these evenings open up like parachutes
and each night someone is saved: by string,
white silk filling with air, snagging on the sky.
But I say these nights fall like card houses
in the wind, the cards swirl at your feet.
A nightlight turns its seashell back to the room.

He walks the few steps
from his life to yours.

He points to the center of Mexico
where he comes from, scratches
an invisible map on the palm of your hand.

This woman he walks up hills with
in San Luis Potosi
is here beside him. Speaks English.

Miguel in Paradise

Love, with an interpreter. Sometimes
the interpreter falls in love by mistake,
the words passing through her like a current,
like a thin blue wire.

A silver ball turns throwing light around the room—
into a dark corner
where a couple sits unnamed
on a grey sofa, into
a strawberry daiquiri tilting
down a young woman's throat.

His stovepipe jeans, worn white in places.

With one look in your eyes, he tries to enter
your country. Each word he speaks
takes him one step further away
from home.

The pattern of our feet across the floor.
If we dance long enough in one place,
it becomes ours.

A yellow wedge of neon
winks above our heads, a false moon.
It is all we have.

When he asks you your name
you think hard, knowing it is something
he will not give back easily.

Tell me a story, he says in English.

You take him to a room where you undo
the long line of black buttons on his sweater.
You tell him the story.

for Jimmi Brown

The Pursuit of Happiness :: Too Good To Be True

1 :: love
Once I was shy and lived
in a shoebox. A caveman,
I marked my days in colored chalk
on a white stucco wall, drew pictures
of happiness in an awkward hand:
a telephone, a haircut,
a new pair of shoes.

But when I found my voice
one day in a second-hand store
wrapped in tinfoil and green ribbon—
everything changed. I became
gregarious as a Fuller Brush man
with a low threshold for loneliness.
And so I entered the Wild World
of Dating.

There was the Saturday morning with Sam
we slipped into his Volkswagen Rabbit
and sped off to the Planetarium
to watch the solar system being born,
star by star. Critical by nature,
we renamed the constellations.
The Big Dipper became Glass Shoe
With Nothing Better To Do.
The Milky Way became Spilt Milk
and we cried and cried in our velvet
seats—even though we'd been told
not to. And we saw in the patterns of light
what would be impossible between us.

2 :: food
I thought I could eat
my way back to happiness,
a caterpillar in its round room
clawing for the door.
And when I knew it wouldn't be
Sam, my South American architect,
taking up my time, spreading
his blueprints on my bureau—
I reached instead for coffee
and all the countries it came from,
swallowed Colombia in a single gulp,

took Bolivia hot and scalding
on my tongue, sent Brazil
a river raging down my throat.

And when the flashing red light
of my answering machine stopped
being a lighthouse for me,
I sought sanctuary in a sea
of spinach and cheddar soup, the crackers,
the sourdough bread, all my little rowboats
of hope.

And so my face became like the moon
and when I walked, it was as if
on wheels.
Everyday in every way, I got wider
and wider. And everything I touched
became circular, became rounder,
smoother, more moon-like—
the moon itself being something
made of cheese. And therefore
edible.

3 :: sex
I step out of the Music Box
Theater where inside
a foreign movie spins from its reel
and try to leave Istanbul
behind me. I step off
the bus and there is Raouf
my friend from Morocco.
"Are you happy?" he inquires,
pinning me against a hurricane fence
with the flashlight of his question.

It is then that I turn
from Raouf and movie screens
all over the world and climb
the damp steps to the fun house
of sex. Inside I am greeted
by a corridor of black booths
and the dim red light of a Coke
machine. It is there inside one booth,
I find Pleasure, the fraternal twin
of Happiness—

one stranger patting my head,
the other rubbing my stomach,
while I sing the Star-Spangled Banner
in Portuguese as a hex
against my unhappiness. I surrender
to the massage of multiple hands
smoothing, polishing
I make my last wish
under a car wash of caresses—
my worries rubbed away
to the nothing they always were.

4 :: adventure
Today I work in market research.
Inside one booth, I find a telephone
to the stars and all the Ticonderoga
#2 pencils I could ever want.

I talk to a woman exterminator
from the Bronx about roach control,
how she feels about poison—
her passion melts the phone,
how she fears the mistakes science
makes, the roach mutations blossoming
under baseboards, the Frankensteins
forming in cracks and crevices
of ordinary homes. She stands
on a soapbox and sings the song
of the Misunderstood Exterminator.

I ask mothers across America what
breakfast cereals they sit down to,
what radio stations they wake up to,
and how many times a week they pretend
their husbands are Tom Selleck
as they rip the Hawaiian shirts
from their backs.

But today, I conduct a survey
of my own:
"On a scale from 1 to 10 where
10 means very happy and 1 means
not happy at all—how would you
rate your life?"
Susan gives her life a 5, tells me

of the last two times she was happy:
the time Renee spun her through
a revolving door and she went skidding
across a polished wood floor
knocking over two waiters and a Ficus tree.
The time her
grandmother gave her a book of everything
she was sure of in life—it was very short.
But when I pass a magic wand
over Susan's head, what does she wish for?
Spiritual advancement.
"To witness something," she explains.
"Like a miracle or something. Like if
some kind of ship came in for me,
or I was discovered to be this
great unknown tap dancer. Or if
someone loved me back. Now that
would be a miracle."

I have wanted to tell you
how nice it is. How some nights
I have a bowl of cereal and dream
and the cornflakes wilt
and I go on dreaming
and my future is as certain as the knife
cutting through the banana.

How some nights my cousin and I talk
for hours on the phone
and the telephones become seashells
in our hands
and we listen to each other
as if listening to the sea.

How a certain young woman and I once
searched for wild mangoes in a city
that knew only apples and oranges
by heart, searched
for the perfect dance frame,
the perfect crime—a scavenger hunt
that always led us back to each other.

I have wanted to draw my life in pencil
so that you would not see the mistakes.
Would not see how much guesswork
is really involved.

How can I tell you about a handshake
that lasted eight years?
About weekends spent
not wisely but too well,
keeping each other out late,
waiting for the bus that would bring us back
to our senses
or at least within walking distance.

How can I tell you about a picnic
on the beach that began and ended with water,
placing the bottles of Perrier
in the sand along the shore
because it was the thing to do,
not knowing how you can lose your bottles
to the ocean if you're not careful,
not knowing how they long to return.

I
have
wanted
to
tell
you
how
nice
it
is

There are many things I have wanted to tell you—
I haven't told you everything. But mostly
I just wanted to tell you how nice it is.
How some nights I have a bowl of cereal
and dream and the cornflakes wilt
and I go on dreaming and my future
is as certain as the knife cutting through
the banana.
But you already know how nice it is.
And even before the words have crossed my mind,
even before I've said it—you've heard.

I
H
A
V
E

W
A
N
T
E
D

T
O

T
E
L
L

Y
O
U

H
O
W

N
I
C
E

I
T

I
S

There is a paint factory I pass on my way home.
One white wall of it faces the sidewalk
and at night young boys take flashlights and spray paint
and tell the wall everything they know:

> LISA S. IS A BITCH
> THIS TOWN IS IN THE TWILIGHT ZONE
> I CAME. I SAW. I LEFT.

**Suburban
Graffiti**

And once a month the owners paint the wall white
and hope.

Sometimes I think I see my name
in the scrawls they leave
of black and blue but no—
it's DOUG or DANNY and I walk on.

I pass by the wall today and look for news:

Sharon loves Phil this month.
Julie and Nick are still together.
Lisa S. is still a bitch.

When the Night Finds You

1 ::
Everything important happens
at night, you said
drawing the shades. Power failures,
elopements, even babies
begin in the dark. Outside
a thunderstorm was starting up.
Under the big top of blue-
and-white striped sheets, I began
my climb, tying the sheets
into one long rope, into the tail
of a kite—I was halfway out the window
when you woke me. You said, what with
the lightning behind me and the
knotted sheet in my hands,
it looked like
I was trying to discover something.

2 ::
Maybe a ventriloquist could breathe
words into me again, his hand
reaching up through a hole in my back.
What I wanted was so small: to be able
to enter any room with a story to tell.
But my legs were wood, they folded
in two, and the words came from a place
behind me.
On stage in our dazzling tuxedos,
it'd be my lips the audience would
be watching, my story
they'd be falling in love with.
Later, after the roses
had been swept into a dustpan,
the ventriloquist would lock me in
a steamer trunk, telling me each night
how lucky I am.

3 ::
Last night, my big brother came to rescue me.
Even by the rhythm of his car rolling up
the drive, even by the way I answered the doorbell
before it rang—we knew
it was an emergency.
An ordinary handkerchief, he is saying
waving out the folds in one sweeping motion,

WHEN THE NIGHT FINDS YOU

holding it by its corners to show me
its lack of mystery. He is letting me see.
I drop the thing to the floor and it takes forever
to fall, floating like milk weed
in an open field. Here, let me do it, he says
bending over the field as if he has lived
all his life outdoors.
He lowers the handkerchief gently over my head.
He whispers my name in my ear
and it stays there. He unveils me.

for Charlene

Here in this room
where many women go under,
die quiet dishwater deaths,
one woman is holding on:
fingers reaching
for buttons and switches
for Pyrex, for Teflon, for Tupperware
all the gods she prayed to
to protect her
for wax paper dreams

Kitchen

folded in with each sandwich
she wraps and sends out
into the world.

She wants to find
a baby on her doorstep
and ask no questions.
She wants to turn to
the man in bed with her and ask
"What have you done with my husband?"
She wants to go back
to her wedding day
and explain.

Instead she leaves a note
under the butter dish.
"To whom it may concern:
My heart, this rented space
with hot and cold running water,
two bedrooms and no children.
You are not who I thought you were."

When she leaves this room, she leaves for good.
She does not bother to push in her chair.

Two men sit blowing on their coffee as they watch
a wrecking ball swing through the walls
of the Stardust Bowling Alley.
Can't understand why people have stopped bowling,
says one. The other
nods, stirring the sugar
at the bottom of his cup.

: :

Mysteries
of
a
Bowling
Alley

It is only Saturday morning and already the city
has lost one bowling alley. By nine o'clock
a string of customers has tied itself
into a knot outside our doors.
So, Laurie, how's life in the fast lane? Richard asks
looping a tie over his head.
Richard, it is so fast...it streaks behind me
and she smiles. We take
our places behind the counter, grinning
as the doors are unlocked and the crowd
pushes in.

: :

To move with direction
we make lists. Draw up agendas and pushpin them
onto bulletin boards:

1) Find a lover
2) Cut my hair
3) Go to Keith's barbeque
4) Fall in bed with someone I like
5) Figure out what's bothering me
6) Hang new pictures on my wall

And sometimes, walking down into another day,
we catch our breath on the stairs.

: :

I've been watching my best friend fall in love.
It's not like watching a leaf fall from a tree—
more like raking leaves in a yard somewhere,

the garbage bag held open by someone you like.
And I wonder what it's like
to be watched
raking leaves.

: :

Closing time: a bus rolls by, green windows heavy
with light and I'm facing the window again
in Arnie's All-Night Snack Shop.
A local crazy ambles up to the glass. He puts
thumb to nose and flutters his fingers at me.
I wave back,
trying to think what fish
he reminds me of.

: :

Joe. That's a simple name remarks a voice
near the video games. I know, another answers,
I've spent my whole life trying to compensate—
And the bar is buzzing with talk:
true love on a Tuesday night but it's Saturday
already and the waiters are counting their tips,
beer bottles flying toward plastic bins and landing
on the floor. You only came to dance,
to wave your body like a flag
in the middle of the floor.

: :

After the rice is thrown, what's left
but two people standing on the sidewalk:
all dressed up and nowhere to go.
So they head for the house, they cross
the threshold.
This is the first time I opened the door,
he thinks.

: :

Simply walk out of one life and into another,
advises the article in the paper.

But I want to be followed—a blue car
parked outside my house, shadows in the hall,
spools of my voice unwinding like thread in a drawer.
I want to be found: alive, on key
in the middle of my song.

: :

You loved bowling for its lack of mystery:
stick three fingers in a ball—
and throw.
But nothing's as simple as that, nothing
is changed with the falling of pins.
You turned your bowling ball into a paperweight
and still important papers blew away.

She sat in front of me all through grade school
because of our names: O'Connor, Ozawa.
I know the back of Denise's head very well.

FAMILY
RESEMBLANCES

They say if you don't
name a child when it is born,
it will start crawling north,
unable to be pulled back
by the string of its name.
It will start the party
without you, without names.

Once on a busy downtown street,
I saw a woman lower
a blue rope around her
two children saying:
"This is for safety.
Because I love you"—
and she pulled the knot closed.
A perfect lasso of love.
And so her children went
in blue orbit around her,
and so wherever they wandered
she could pull them back
by the string of their names.

Or perhaps they had
no names. And so
she bound them tight
with ropes, afraid they
would go spinning away from her,
without names,
       without ropes,
         away.

**Poem
for
the
Unnamed**

In Response to Executive Order 9066 :: All Americans of Japanese Descent Must Report to Relocation Centers

Dear Sirs:
Of course I'll come. I've packed my galoshes
and three packets of tomato seeds. Denise calls them
love apples. My father says where we're going
they won't grow.

I am a fourteen-year-old girl with bad spelling
and a messy room. If it helps any, I will tell you
I have always felt funny using chopsticks
and my favorite food is hot dogs.
My best friend is a white girl named Denise —
we look at boys together. She sat in front of me
all through grade school because of our names:
O'Connor, Ozawa. I know the back of Denise's head very well.

I tell her she's going bald. She tells me I copy on tests.
We're best friends.

I saw Denise today in Geography class.
She was sitting on the other side of the room.
"You're trying to start a war," she said, "giving secrets
away to the Enemy, Why can't you keep your big
mouth shut?"

I didn't know what to say.
I gave her a packet of tomato seeds
and asked her to plant them for me, told her
when the first tomato ripened
she'd miss me.

Notes
for
a
Poem
on
Being
Asian
American

As a child, I was a fussy eater
and I would separate the yolk from the egg white
as I now try to sort out what is Asian
in me from what is American—
the east from the west, the dreamer from the dream.
But countries are not
like eggs — except in the fragileness
of their shells — and eggs resemble countries
only in that when you crack one open and look inside,
you know even less than when you started.

And so I crack open the egg,
and this is what I see:
two moments from my past that strike me
as being uniquely Asian American.

In the first, I'm walking down Michigan Avenue
one day — a man comes up to me out of the blue and says:
"I just wanted to tell you...I was on the plane that
bombed Hiroshima. And I just wanted you to know that
what we did was for the good of everyone." And it
seems as if he's asking for my forgiveness. It's 1983,
there's a sale on Marimekko sheets at the Crate &
Barrel, it's a beautiful summer day and I'm talking to
a man I've never seen before and will probably never
see again. His statement has no connection to me —
and has every connection in the world. But it's not
for me to forgive him. He must forgive himself.
"It must have been a very difficult decision to do what
you did," I say and I mention the sale on Marimekko
sheets across the street, comforters, and how the
pillowcases have the pattern of wheat printed on them,
and how some nights if you hold them before an open
window to the breeze, they might seem like flags —
like someone surrendering after a great while, or
celebrating, or simply cooling themselves in the summer
breeze as best they can.

In the second moment — I'm in a taxi and the Iranian
cabdriver looking into the rearview mirror notices my
Asian eyes, those almond shapes, reflected in the glass
and says, "Can you really tell the difference between
a Chinese and a Japanese?"

And I look at his 3rd World face, his photo I.D. pinned
to the dashboard like a medal, and I think of the eggs
we try to separate, the miles from home he is and the
minutes from home I am, and I want to say: "I think
it's more important to find the similarities between
people than the differences." But instead I simply
look into the mirror, into his beautiful 3rd World
eyes, and say, "Mr. Cabdriver, I can barely tell the
difference between you and me."

1 :: letter to a friend who left
Dear David,
Last week when I ordered a hot turkey sub to go,
your Iranian friend working behind the counter
told me you died as he was giving me my change.
I can still hear the quarters fall,
hitting the floor with a metal sound. They bounced
I think. Funny
how things slip through your fingers.
I am trying to say goodbye.
I'm trying to wave my hand just so.
To look at your Robert Fripp album spinning
on my stereo and imagine how far away
you must be.

I didn't believe you
when you said you loved me at the bar.
I said you were drunk.
I pushed your hat over your eyes. I am trying
to lift your hat back up. I am trying to say
I love you too.

2 :: to my brother in the basement
Clyde,
In the lowest room in the house where cold air sinks
and TV voices go rising through the vents, I find you
watching the Late Show, wearing my shirt.
Happy, aren't you? I ask, staring into the
screen's flickering blue—Fred Astaire dances there
on a dining room table.
What's happy? you say flipping the channel,
past talk shows and Pontiac dealers.
There is no secret you know of.

But I see you slipping out the back way
with your camera for a midnight shoot with friends.
I hear you sneak back in, the creaking floor
announcing your return. I'm through
watching test patterns on TV.
I want to dance on the dining room table
like everyone else.

Letters I Never Wrote

3 :: to a woman on a bench
Ma'am,
We have never met before.
I send this letter as a gesture, the way
a boy aims a paper plane at the moon.
I have read in the paper of your sad story—
how you found the gun too heavy to lift
and hired someone to move the bullet
into your head.
The night before, you threw a party for friends,
said you were going away. Minneapolis? California?
Kalamazoo? They wanted to know.
I'll write, you promised pouring the tea
into sand-colored cups.

That last moment in the park, you looked hard
at the trees. You wanted to remember what trees were.
It was a Saturday, you wore your favorite
navy blue dress, a man stands near the fountain,
you love your brother in Arkansas,
the leaves fall faster,
the man nods at you.

4 :: an invitation to another life
Dear Cousin Ron,
I write to tell you of life in the next room.
Those party sounds seeping under your door
last night—I made them. The champagne glass
that rolled under the blue couch
was mine. You're invited to a party.
There's ice
in the freezer,
champagne in the shower stall.
You'll wake from a night of tossing
with confetti in your hair.

When you turned around last fall
and best friend had run off to Canada
with your car, you said you wouldn't
trust anyone anymore.
I give up, you said pushing the world away
with both hands.
Enough already. I'm tired of blowing up balloons
for people I don't know. Come to my party.

5 :: letter from my Dark Ages

Dear Dwight,
I'm writing to you from five years ago.
Hope you're standing near a lamp because
this is a letter from your Dark Ages.
I suffer from nightmares. In one, I'm sitting
on a train. A boy taps on the window:
Take me with you, he pleads through the green glass.
He looks exactly like me. There's no room, I say.
All the tickets have been sold.
He raises his suitcases high over his head.
He tries to fly.

This morning, the train was gone. My mother
was sitting on a lawnchair in the backyard,
the Daily News in her lap. I could tell
she was looking at the world.
What is this trick she's learned
of standing in natural light, stepping through a hoop
and coming out golden, coming out doves?
Teach it to me, I say. I will practice it
in the spare room till I am good.
But she just keeps singing.

LETTERS I NEVER WROTE

It was a picnic where they first laid eyes
"Maybe it was my hair that made him look"
My mother shrugs back thirty years and sighs
My father snores, his hands around a book

"He brought me napkins when the food was served
My skirt was green and flared around my knees"
Under the weight of rice, their paper plates curved
They sat, two people meeting under trees

My
Parents

: :

How
They
Met

"I guess it was my hair, I had it done—
short in back and curly on the top"
She runs a finger where a curl would be
Father stirs, the book he's holding drops

He rises now and climbs the stairs these nights
They meet again beneath ceilings painted white.

We're Given a Father For Such A Short Time

I walk out onto the dock
as far as I can go in the rain,
the rain with its many arrows
pointing to the earth
where you have gone
fishing. I wonder what it was
you loved about fishing,
had nothing to do with fish.
Had more to do with the lake.
How in those long stretches
of time you became son
to the lake and it raised you,
loved you back with its waves
and water, its shiny blue fish.

In Buddhism, we believe
in Cause and Effect. You can't leave
one place without arriving
some place else
Here's to your safe arrival—
wherever that is. Here's to
the universe that gave me a father
for such a short time.
"Here, take Fred. But give him back
when you're done." When you're done
doing the things that angels do
with fathers that fish.
Tell jokes about The One That Got Away,
spin him around three times
till he walks back confused
in another direction, another life,
becomes my barber, my busybody neighbor,
my best friend.

Pin the tail on your life.
Recognize it from a speeding car.
Here's to the car that gets you there.
Here's to the traffic that gets
in your way.

If my mother wants to go
to Japan, I do too.
So I pencil my time away
in charcoal slashes.
So I mark my calendar with
a haystack of days.

She wanted to go with my father—to stand
knee-deep in rice paddies at dawn
as she waded through wheat fields
of Nebraska on their last big trip west.

If My Mother Wants to Go to Japan

But my father went before her,
alone, into a country not named
and not Japan.
He went on ahead to meet her,
to wait up for her.
In love, two people go through doors
together. If they love each other
they wait.

So my father waits.
So my father takes his long
afternoon nap.

If my mother wants to go to Japan,
I do too. So I buy a house in the air
and a 1,000 yen bill dusted
with pastel inks. I pay a high price
for that currency—twice what
my brother paid.

I eat ricecakes piled high
with tuna and cream cheese.
I remove my shoes.
I go to Japan. I take my mother
with me.

1 :: the art of shopping

It began with a foot
touching bottom and
the door flying open.
Magic from the word go.

From then on, we talk
in a language of food
and know each other's mouth
like the back of our hands.

Reaching for a carton of eggs,
I see a hand slamming down
against a frying pan's edge.
You squeeze a melon
and juice comes drooling down
as my knife slides in.

Between raisin bread and rye, however,
our sympathies divide—
we see the lever being lowered,
the toaster thinking in its warm way...
Aw, c'mon, you say
and I weaken.

Talk to me in that
peanut-butter-and-jelly tone of voice.
Read me you shopping list
like you mean it.
And if we never live together again,
let's always shop together—

clank our carts down the same aisle,
find time to stand in line.
We cannot see beyond next week's
shopping list. We do not even try.

2 :: the art of flirting

The aquarium in the window tells me
I have arrived, but the waiter
in the leather apron smiling
tells me more.
Tells me there are many fish
in the sea, tells me
bedtime stories with his eyes and I listen...

Lost
Arts
of
the
20th
Century

through glass, through oceans, I listen
and the catfish turn away.

Sometimes it is like
bidding at an auction:
a tug on an ear lobe,
a folding of arms across a chest,
an uncrossing of legs.

Sometimes it is like
kissing in the dark and so
we picture it in our heads:
waking up each morning
to this new face—
this mouth, this laugh.

Sad to say in matters of the heart
he is only the messenger.
Not the recipient of all this good news.

At the Waterfront Restaurant
where they grow waiters
as tempting as their seafood,
the leather apron takes a message:
Tell Bruce I miss him
and you're not so bad yourself.

3 :: the art of holding on
So this is Monday.
I open my door and there it is
with the mail: ready, waiting.
And if I step into it like a taxi
will it take me somewhere,
can I roll down the windows
and shout my name as loud as it'll go?
I open my hand and feel for rain,
I climb in.
Here we go, hold on.

Marcie slips into Wednesday
like a new dress. It flatters her
and she looks on the bright side,
looks at a map and wonders where
her priorities lie: All these roads.
But by evening she's there

and she can count on one finger
all the reasons she came.

Frank likes his Fridays, wants
to hold them in his hands
like pencils and see if they write.
Tonight he'll call me out of the blue
and tell me he's made plans for the evening
and I am part of them: See you at 6:00.
The day spins on its edge
and drops like a penny
to the sidewalk—call it.
Heads.

A poem is wonderful because you can take a moment of your life and spin it around in a million different directions. But with a play, you could take a year of your life and connect all the dots...

Smuggling Poetry into the Theater

1 :: DREAM/FAST

If I knew tomorrow was gonna be the end of the world, I think I'd go swimming. I'd borrow Sam's goggles and swim till I was blue in the gills, blue as the deep blue sea I was swimming in. I'd backstroke my way through the world. Tell the sun and moon: "Good night, thanks for the light." I'd swim away from everything that ever hurt me, and I'd swim toward everything that ever loved me back...Sam, Juanita, my parents, Buddhism, poetry. I'd keep swimming till I became part of the sea, happy and blue. Then I'd evaporate into thin air. I'd be just this little breeze blowing across the face of the earth.

2 :: The Rainy Season

In my country, we have a time of year—in your time, it would be somewhere between spring and summer. We call it: "the rainy season." At first, we have drizzles, then monsoons. The rains are so heavy...cities flood, cars float like toys in the street. Or there is a mud slide and a house vanishes overnight. It's a dangerous time—anything can happen. A study has shown more people fall in love during the rainy season than any other time of year. I think because it is the one time of year we realize how alone we are, how alone we have always been. And so, we turn to each other. We give in. We surrender to all that we know...in the rainy season.

3 :: Letters I Never Wrote

To Whom It May Concern:
I don't know if you'll get this letter. Just because I wrote it—doesn't guarantee anything. But I did finally write a letter down, and that's a start. People walk around all the time with letters inside them they never write or send, and that's not healthy. It just weighs a person down I think. Sometimes I wonder what letters must be floating around inside you. My Dad and I are finally leaving this stupid relocation camp for good. They say the war may be ending soon. We're moving to Chicago where we don't know anyone. When we get there, I just wanna soak in a tub of hot water till I'm a giant prune. When I dry off, I'll be a new person. Maybe I'll even be an American—whatever that is. At any rate, it's been two of the most interesting years of my life. Maybe someday, when we're not so mad at each other, we can talk about it.

for Yoshio and Takeyo Okita

"In the hot summers of the 30's, we would
sit on the steps and sing for hours. We
even counted the stars in the sky and it
was always beautiful."

So my mother begins
writing her life down, Jackie Onassis
thinking in the car behind dark glasses.
She recalls the luxury
of growing up—she and her sisters

**The
Nice
Thing
About
Counting
Stars**

buying jelly bismarcks on Sundays
and eating them in the back seat
of their father's Packard
parked on the drive.
Pretending they were going
somewhere, and they were.
Not knowing years later they would
be headed for just such an exotic place.
Somewhere far from Fresno, their white stone house
on F Street, the blackboard in the kitchen
where they learned math,
long division, remainders,
what is left
after you divide something.

"When Executive Order 9066 came telling
all Japanese-Americans to leave their
houses, we cleared out of Fresno real
fast. They gave us three days. I remember
carrying a washboard to the camp. I don't
know how it got in my hands. Someone must
have told me—Here, take this."

They were given three days to move
what had taken them years to acquire—
sewing machines, refrigerators, pianos, expensive fishing
rods from Italy. A war was on—Japs
had bombed Pearl Harbor.

Burmashave signs littered the highways:

SLAP

THE JAP

"Take only what you can carry."
My mother's family left the Packard
and with it left Sundays in the back seat.
Others walked away from acres of land,
drugstores, photo albums.

I think of turtles.
How they carry their whole lives
on their backs. My neighbor Jimmi
told me one night how they
make turtle soup down south.
A huge sea turtle—take a sledge hammer
to the massive shell, wedge it open
with one simple, solid blow
till the turtle can feel
no home above him, till everything
is taken away
and there is nothing
he will carry away from this moment.

My parents had three days
to relocate.
"Take only what you can carry."
One simple, solid blow—
They felt no home above them.

> "We were sent to Jerome, Arkansas.
> Arriving there, I wondered how long
> we would be fenced in."

The nice thing about counting stars is
you can do it just about anywhere.
Even in a relocation camp
miles from home, even in Jerome, Arkansas
where a barbed wire fence crisscrosses itself
making stars of its own—but nothing
worth counting, nothing worth singing to.

My father remembers only two things:

> washing dishes in the mess hall each morning
> beside George Kaminishi and

> listening to Bing Crosby sing "White Christmas"
> on the radio in the barracks late at night.

One morning, George looked up from a greasy skillet
at my dad and said Yosh, you're a happy-go-lucky guy.
What do you want to do with your life?
It was the first time he realized he had a life
to do things with. He was fifteen. He didn't know.
It was only later that Dad found out George
had colon cancer and had no life to do things with.
And when Bing sang "White Christmas" late at night
Dad could only think, He's not singing to me he's
singing to white people.

My mother meanwhile was in a different camp
and hadn't met my father. At night, she'd lie
in bed and think about the old family car
back in the driveway—were the windows smashed
and broken into, the thing driven away by thieves?

Or was the grass a foot tall now, erasing the
Goodyear tires that were so shiny and new?
There was a hole in the week where Sunday
used to be, and she wanted jelly bismarcks
more than ever.

> "Somehow we adjusted. There were weekly
> dances for the young. Dad sent away
> for a huge rice paper umbrella of vivid colors,
> and Peg and I hugged it during stormy
> days."

Note: Quoted excerpts are from my mother Patsy Takeyo Okita's memoirs.

She's been made to stand naked
in windows, waiting for her clothes
as they formed on sketch pads
under the drag of the designer's pencil.
She has sat in cardboard boxes
at the warehouse, bent at the waist,
spiders binding her feet with silk.

Facing the Mannequin

Now she is tired of all this.
She wants to open her plastic mouth and speak,
of the mannequin's life:
a life of entrances into rooms she cannot love,
how she is allowed only one gesture a month
to convey everything, how when women
hail taxis at night they become still
and they remind her of herself.

: :

There is a fine line between the mannequin
and me and I draw it everyday. But sometimes
I sit in a chair too long, get lost
in thoughts of my ordinary life.
I recognize a gesture of mine in a window
and it startles me, consider
climbing up there to take it back.

But I am more than the gestures I make.

: :

We eye each other through the glass,
enter a poker game in which our faces
give nothing away. I look at the patio
she is standing in, its lawnchairs and barbeque,
her calm in the middle of any meal.

She sees how the sidewalk extends
beyond the frame of her window,
the way my shirt moves when I breathe.

Stay with me in this parking lot,
the driver would say.
All my life, I have held this space
for someone like you.

MEN
IN
LOVE

1 :: Making Coffee
The first time I come over,
you show me a flipbook of your father
when he was a boy. You flip the pages
and the boy begins to run,
his Schnauser barking after him.
They fill up the field
with their playing. It makes you
want to join them.

Sometimes all you can do is watch,
I say. Sometimes a man runs through a field
and never looks back.
You boil a pan of water
at the stove, shovel instant coffee
into glass mugs letting the spoons
clink on the bottom.

My father owns a flower shop, you say.
He has a bad heart, but it's in
the right place.
And the water is hot enough. You pour it bubbling
into our cups. Making coffee
gives us something to do with our hands
as we get to know each other,
as I eye the sofa bed I want to pull you toward.

2 :: Driving the Car
When I introduced you to Klee,
I knew you'd like her
and we took midnight drives
along the lake, pulling the moon
behind us like a balloon.
You, me, and Klee jammed into the front seat,
an ordinary family traveling across America
in a straight line.

One night we spread a sheet on Klee's floor
and pretended to be roommates. We fell asleep
in front of the TV with Johnny Carson
waving his hands, fell asleep
to the sound of applause.

In the night, I heard sounds—
kissing, breathing, sucking, breathing

**When
Frank
Walks
In**

I watched you make love to her
on the floor inches from my face. I pretended
to be asleep, to be watching TV in my dreams,
but I was watching you.

Did I tell you the sound you made
was the sound a weightlifter makes
when he presses 200 pounds over his head,
so out of breath like that?
How there was nothing on TV
and still I kept watching?

3 :: Marking the Place

The day you moved away I saw coming.
I dreamed I woke
and my friends had scattered
across a pastel map of fifty states.

                    Start again, a voice said.

You locked your arm
around my neck claiming me
before the passing cars,
the driver/witnesses already
disappearing in their mirrors.
Streetlights leaned closer,
children dropped pennies down
drainage grates where all good things go.

We said goodbye at the elevator
while upstairs moving men
circled your mahogany table
with green quilts in their hands.

                    Capture it in a net.

It was a pleasure
making breakfast for you, you told me.
I'll never forget your shoes,
how heavy they were.

                    Set it free.

I think of the night we walked
to the Lincoln Park Lagoon,

to the dock shaped like an X
on the water as if it marked where
something was.
I threw a quarter into the lagoon.
I spent my money. I spent it all
in one place. And the two of us
lay down on the splintering wood
to be examined by the stars.

Angel at the Train Station

My train pulls in at dusk,
that powder-blue place
between day and night.
His red Camaro parked square
in front of the station door
so no one can come or go
without wondering who
is waiting inside that car.

At each stop light, I kiss his arms.
They're hard from lifting
boxes of nails all day from
one conveyor belt to another.
The skin on his arms is smooth
as peach skin, the fine hairs
polishing my lips.

Say this is the man I have always wanted,
the one I have waited for
at crosswalks. Say, he is
the beautiful one I saw in my dream
last night taking off his shirt,
unbuttoning each white button
until there were no more buttons
and he stood naked under a shower nozzle,
the water washing over his body,
polishing him in the bright light
that found him.

All night, he makes me think of clouds
and floating things.

All night, he moves me
from one conveyor belt
to another.

Somewhere in Chicago, a woman unplugs a toaster
from a wall and suddenly her apartment is empty.
She wraps the cord, jumprope-style, into a bow,
lowers the appliance into a box marked:
"Kitchen Things" and tapes it shut.
All day boxes move past her, a brown blur
against the white walls.
How many men does it take
to lift a woman's spirits?

: :

The Farewell Samba

Make your arms like a barrel
I scolded, your dance instructor,
fox-trotting you around the room.
Women are always walking backwards,
aren't they? you said looking at your feet
and I spun you.
No, just going in circles
and here we laughed. In the mirrors
of the dance studio we laughed
and I saw us: Lost in the Fun House again.
I want it always to be fun.

: :

Now everything is loaded on the truck.
She sits behind the wheel of something
larger than her. I'm going to Timbuktu
and I am taking my time, she says,
her hands on the wheel. Peaches, pears,
apples, plums—tell me when your birthday comes,
and I wave to her from the curb.
It paints a sad picture, this:
Woman in Van Pulling out of a Driveway No Longer Hers.
And for her,
I do a farewell samba on the lawn, alone
taking the darkness in the crescent of my arms,
leading it in a dance I am just beginning
to learn.

Last night, John and I
went to sleep talking about
the tattoos we'd leave
on each other. Anchors, eagles—no,
not the ordinary things.
For him, I wanted an airplane
gliding across his left thigh.
For me, he saw a parachutist
coming down across the sky of my chest.
And we called each other
merciless in our planning.
And we could be spoons in bed,
sky to sky—the parachutist
and the plane he left.
In the morning, it made no difference.
We woke late, tattooless,
more naked than ever.

Some Tattoos

: :

He had the sun tattooed
on his chest, I had the moon
and when we made love face to face,
we called it an eclipse.
The blue shadows we cast
on the bed below us, the sunglasses
we wore to look at each other.
And when you put your weight
on me, when the room went dark
and vast—it was hard
not to hear the planets whirring,
the stars coming on, hard to imagine
a time before Sun and Moon, this
eclipse.

: :

When we leave the bar
they stamp our hands with
a rubber stamp and for a moment
we are passports—why shouldn't
our bodies say so? But even
when they stamp a navy blue eagle
on your wrist as if to say
the door is open, fly right in—

you can never come back.
Better to drown the eagle
in warm soap and water, better
to forget the places you have been
that mark you, that change you,
that leave you standing at
a bathroom sink at 4 a.m.
rubbing pictures from your hands.

1 :: The Nightmare
It was the year Madonna
came into public view
and left her bellybutton print in cement
in front of Grauman's Chinese Theatre.

But it's the nightmare
I keep remembering
of boys falling from trees,
from the sky.
Boys landing in construction sites,
quarries, on top of buses, at intersections
where the lights go green all at once.

Turn your head to cough
and 5,000 boys fall from the sky.
It's frightening. Light candles
in Central Park to their shadows
falling all night. Push them back
into heaven with our little flames.

2 :: The Media
I met a man named Bruce
at an AIDS conference
who was getting better. TV cameras
closed in on him, lenses sparkling
with good news, they held him up
to the nation as a symbol of hope.
He's dead now.

And I read in the paper about Jim—
a man from Texas who has AIDS.
When he was little, his concept of heaven
was a canasta game with lots of coffee and cigarettes.
But recently in the shower,
he found a maroon splotch on his arm.
Maroon, like a color they leave somewhere.

And now heaven seems closer somehow.
He can almost hear the shuffling of cards
from somewhere high up and far away.

**Where
The
Boys
Were**

3 :: A Man Chooses His Funeral Urn

Sometimes a man sits down on stone steps
beside the pink and brown jar
which will contain him. It could be
a teapot, but there's no spout. He's dying.
He sits down in the middle of the stone steps
as if in the middle of his life.
Lifts the lid,
the pretty bubblegum pink ceramic urn
with brown Japanese strokes
swirled in. He lifts the lid
and looks deep into it:

So this is where I'm headed.
So this will be my new home.

He's tired, he wants
to rest his thinning legs.
Wants to hold
that pink and brown teapot
gently in his hands, as it will one day
hold him. Whisper something
sweet and funny into the empty space
so that he will not be alone
when he gets there.
A nickname. Baby Doll.

4 :: Voice

When they look at my life
like a charcoal sketch
ripped from a pad, tell them
I wasn't done.
That there was color to be added—
oranges, pinks, greys.
That all the lines would eventually lead
toward the horizon, some vanishing
point past the paper's edge.

Tell them how finally
there was nothing left of me:
I ran out of dance steps on a crowded floor,
the parquet wood cracked
beneath my feet.

How I threw my name into the air
and it came down faded ticker tape,
unreadable.

I suppose I'll come hurtling down
from heaven, handsome again. Let me fall
where no one will find me
so you can go on with your life—
a wedge of honeydew melon rocking on a plate.
Pretend it's a bad dream.
Wake up from it.
Wake up from it as I could not.

Went over to Frank's house last night.
We sat on the sofa and peeled oranges,
talked about life, watched TV.
That how you eat oranges? Frank asked me
during a commercial.
Yes, Frank. This is how I do it.
Sometimes all I want is to sit on the sofa
and talk with Frank about anything.

: :

What We Talk About When We Talk About Nothing

I was washing my face when you called
last night. My hands were on faucets,
my mind was on water
and father's voice was lost
in the carpet and the curtains.
That night I walked in my sleep
reached for a towel like a telephone: no answer
and turned off the light.

But tonight is a different story.
Tell it to me in your own words.

1 :: Walking Away

My brother never said he was
leaving home. He just left—
piece by piece.
One night, a floor lamp tucked
under his arm, another night
all his Benny Goodman records
in a box. A mattress here,
a pillow there.
And so a life is dismantled.
Somewhere a life assembles
on the other side—somewhere
boxes opening with a sigh.

My own departure was different
with its many announcings:
T-shirts flung in anger
against a wall, door slammings,
denials. My idle threats
of leaving in the night
while my mother tossed in bed,
her bristly curlers leaving scars
on the pillow.

But then something happened.
The long bar of light under her door,
her pacing in the garden.
She was making up her mind,
tulips knocking their heads
against the hem of her dress.

You're not losing a son, you're gaining
a sewing room, I told her. Yellow tulips
the color of melting butter.
And she liked the idea
of a sewing room. My mother,
so easily persuaded.

2 :: The New Place

The first night, I take
a long stroll across the maroon
shag rug of my apartment.
Once this was a hotel. Bellboys
in red caps opened their palms
to whatever was coming to them.

White stucco walls like frosting
on a cake, the arched doorways—
all that drama.
How many honeymoon couples
passed under them?
And with each arch I pass under
I think to myself: I am on my way.

Prove yourself to those
who watch you from small windows
no bigger than your hand. Mothers
who carry your picture at the front
of their wallets, mothers everywhere
with rooms to rent.

::

I stand on a wooden chair to hang it
upside down from the kitchen
ceiling—a rice paper umbrella
with a turquoise peacock painted
on it. A motor
turns it round and round and so
the peacock flies
in slow circles above my head.
It hovers over me
for days, circling.

I picture the housewarming
party I will throw, see
myself draping pastel streamers
from the umbrella spokes,
streamers dusting the air.

On one white wall, a 3' x 3' poster
dominates with a huge glass bath house
from the turn
of the century. Men on the dock
with dark green swimsuits
cross their arms, defying
the photographer. Sometimes
I join them there
on the dock. Sometimes I am one
of them, one of the watchers
who sees life as if
from a great distance.

THE LIFE I'M WALKING TOWARD

3 :: My Neighbor

Kathy Carter in Apt. 108 doesn't know
what to do with her brother.
He went through a big depression
when he was little, she says.
It put a dent in him.

It's the Tin Can Theory
of the human soul, the notion
that every blow leaves its mark—
and Kathy Carter subscribes to it.
This is the same brother
who used to catch snakes in a pillowcase,
hanging them like tinsel
from the Aspen tree out back.
Tinsel that moves.

At 4 a.m. last night, she
charged the hallway, fire extinguisher
in hand, spraying away the men
who followed her home from the Octagon.
She knocked at my door—
I opened on a snowstorm of carbon dioxide
cold and white she was laughing
her girlfriend naked
in a puddle on the floor
Kathy Carter
choosing this moment to tell me
she wants to die in a remarkable way
in a space capsule slamming hard
into a fist of earth how
her mother lived in a Dodge Dart
for a year her brother sleeping
in a tent under a starless California
sky

Why shouldn't she wake up on a rooftop
with a cab driver named Yahtzee?
Why shouldn't every blow
leave its mark?

4 :: What the Wall Says

DREAM/FAST
I don't
know why I like this

I just know that in October
the lot fills with pumpkins
and in December with Christmas trees—
old men with dollar bills wrapped
tightly in rubber bands moving
through the lot—and once
I saw a photograph of a man waving
from inside a Winnebago camper
which was parked on the lot
and still the wall behind him said:

DREAM/FAST

It was only when I walked
in front of the wall,
it was only when I put myself
at the center of it,
that I could see myself blurring.
All the Halloweens, the Christmases,
all the Winnebagos
just walked past like that
in one sweeping motion.

5 :: Dark Days
On dark days, I join hands
with the Disenchanted. I watch TV
and the weekends fly.
The umbrella turns,
it carries me away
from my problems,
away from the gorgeous pink hands
of those who love me.
The blue peacock gliding
in mad circles over the
butcher block table—a propeller,
a special wind
that lifts me up
out of my wooden chair,
out of this life where nothing
happens.

                    : :

The distance I travel
from my chair to the TV set
is immense. I will never get there.

But Howie Mandell on the
David Letterman Show is so lovely—
he is a magnet, the way he draws
people to him with his funny stories,
his Silly Putty grin.

: :

At a party, my shyness floats up
like pollen, spores—
they cover everything. Pink waves churn in the
punchbowl: I'm tired of meeting new people,
I confess. New bubbles to burst. Balloon life,
Buddhists call it. Something that pops.

I dance till dawn
to prove I can still be happy—
even if only for these scattered moments
when I'm lifting into the air
and turning, my white gym shoes
blinding even my most Latin admirers.

: :

This barren refrigerator,
the countless wire racks. I want
to crawl inside it
and go to sleep among the cucumbers
and the corn.
I will have my way.
I have already started.

It's continuity I reach for
in bottomless wooden drawers—
one day connected to the next
in a meaningful way, one life
joined to another
in a paper clip chain.

: :

I buy green bananas
and put them on a rattan tray.
I watch them
bring yellow into this house,

a brightness.
I wish I could do that,
whatever the place.

It's a gift, my mother says
her voice sparkling
in hushes
of light.

But I think
it was never given
to me.

6 :: Outside
My mother and I stand
outside my building,
the grey marble columns,
Father circling the block
in a blue Buick.
I have to go, I tell her.
I have things to do.

Don't be so hard on yourself,
she tells me, her voice
a tendril curling up
to brush my ear.

She wants her happy-go-lucky son
back, but it was never that way:

not in the mayonnaise jars
I kept when I was small to smother
fireflies in, jealous of their light,
not in the trees I climbed to get away
each night under a wash of stars,
not in the wordlessness, my mother and I
standing at the window
watching it rain

the rain saying more

than I

could ever say.

7 :: Opening

Tonight I open
my apartment door
as if for the first time.
I open the palm
of my hand to receive the night
in its many disguises.

And the night moves in.

:::

In three hours, I will stand
under a wooden arch at a smoky bar
and wait for a man from Chihuahua, Mexico
to give me a sign. I'll take him to
a sofa so blue we'll swim in it,
into the years of waiting
which are also blue.
We will go places in that sofa.
Maybe, we will come back.

Happiness takes you
by the hand, sits you down
in a plain blue chair and tells you
what you want to know.

You really want to, huh?
You really want to do it?
But he is already asleep, breathing
the deep sleep of another place,
already rounding third base
for the long run home, baseball caps
sailing into the air.

8 :: Now

I don't know what happens now.
I'll tune in next week
along with the rest of us.
I just know what Keith told me
about ribbons, that there comes
a point in your life
when all the ribbons you made
come together

and this is the life

I'm walking toward.

Already the sky has forgotten everything:
how to darken its picture,
how to draw circles around the moon,
the proper spacing of the stars.

It's always this way, he says.
First the stars go, then the year,
fading like the white dot
after the TV's been turned off.

Etch

-a-

Sketch

And once a year
we shake it loose the sky,
our Etch-a-Sketch plans—
all the people that didn't last,
all the glue that didn't hold,
rainchecks, rendezvous, everything
that fell through.

I pushed open the door
that held me there and ran
headlong into the new year.

All these nights, all these traffic lights.
And love, that busy street.

And scientists would stand in white coats and talk
amongst themselves about the Doppler Effect:
how love takes longer to arrive than to depart,
a car approaching in the oncoming lane, what happens
when source and observer are drawing closer together.

Crossing
with
the
Light

And poets would see love in the parking of a car,
love in the rear-view mirror, love in the slowing
of tires between yellow lines.
"Stay with me in this parking lot," the driver
would say. "All my life, I have held this space
for someone like you."

Meanwhile back at the curb,
we were waiting.

I wanted to stand here and watch
the city run out of things to say
and the cars out of gas
till everything was stopped—
and you would be the first thing to move.

But nights like these, you can look both ways
and still not see it coming. Nights like these
you want to walk away from headlights.

Meanwhile back at the curb...
we were crossing, shoes lifting
over pavement, steady as rain:
"Red Rover, Red Rover, let..."
That someone would be waiting on the other side—
not waiting to cross, not waiting for signs,
waiting only for you this time.

Something in your stride asks,
"This one? This time? Is this it?"

And a voice that comes from the street,
from the cracks in the sidewalk,
from the curb you stand on and all the curbs
you've ever stood on and waited at—
a voice that says, "Yes.
This one. This time. This is the place."